MARKET!

Ted Lewin

Market!

LOTHROP, LEE & SHEPARD BOOKS
NEW YORK

A NOTE FROM THE AUTHOR

FROM THE CHILL HIGHLANDS OF THE ANDES TO THE steamy jungles of central Africa, from the fabled souks of Morocco to the tough New York waterfront, people come to market.

They come barefoot and bent with backbreaking loads, walking for days over lonely mountain passes. They come on jungle trails and roads jammed with traffic. They come by dugout canoe from upriver or by trawler after weeks away at sea. They come any way they can.

They come to sell what they grow, catch, or make, and to buy what other people grow, catch, or make.

So come along—let's go to market!

TO SUSAN PEARSON

ECUADOR
SAQUISILI, NEAR AMBATO

They come, descendants of the Incas, as colorful as tulips with names like Salasacas and Chimborazo. They bring their onions and bitter potatoes grown on terraced slopes that step into the clouds.

They bring their sweaters and ponchos made from the wool of sheep and llamas. Tailors set up shop right on the spot.

They bring bowls made of used tires, and sharp, cane-cutting knives in the shape of crescent moons. They bring rope made of sisal and reeds for thatching. The spice seller takes on the colors of the spices he sells out of old paint cans.

NEPAL
PATAN, NEAR KATHMANDU

They have come for a thousand years over rugged mountain passes, bearing heavy loads held by tumplines on their foreheads or in baskets on poles slung across their shoulders. They bring loads of thatch, potatoes, long radishes and chili peppers, garlic, scallions, sugarcane, and ginger. They set out their balance scales and are ready for business.

Durbar Square bustles with bicycles and motor bikes, holy men and holy cows, people making quiet offerings at elaborately carved shrines, and vendors selling wood carvings, wool carpets, and copper pots.

In the square behind the flute sellers, the temples rise to the sky. The mountains beyond rise like white battlements.

IRELAND

BALLINASLOE, COUNTY GALWAY

They come under wet lead skies, in barrel-shaped wagons as colorful as lacquered Russian boxes. Tough, horse-trading men and fortune-telling women, the Gypsies come with their wealth on the hoof: quick, lean trotters and heavy piebald beauties with round, feathered feet and mad blue eyes.

They camp on the hill beneath the church and sell their horses on the steep, stone steps leading down to the green. Crowded together, the horses are wild and skittish and dangerous.

To show off their horses, the men fluff their feathers with sawdust or ride them bareback down the concrete strip at the foot of the steps, right into the crowd.

A farrier hammers musically on a glowing red horseshoe:

Da da dingdingding
Dingdang
Dingdang
Brrrrringding ding!

The farmers come too—out onto the green as big as four football fields—with big red hunters and shaggy donkeys, Irish draughts, fine-lined jumpers, and tiny Shetland ponies.

The milling sea of horses churns the green into thick, pungent muck. It seems as though all the horses in the world are here: chestnuts, sorrels, bays, blacks, grays. When the sun breaks through, the whites and piebalds dazzle. From the hill above, they look like a great army about to charge into battle.

UGANDA
NEAR KABALEGA FALLS

On a dirt road through the rain forest beneath the Mountains of the Moon, they come. They lead their cows to slaughter, then sell the meat on palm-leaf counters.

They bring tiny bananas, apples, tomatoes, and fat limes, and stack them in neat pyramids under corrugated tin roofs.

They bring smoked fish—big Nile perch—caught at the great Kabalega Falls, near the source of the White Nile.

At the end of the day, all that's left at this crossroad are empty sheds and blood-stained palm leaves.

United States
Fulton Fish Market, New York City

They come while most of us are sleeping, by truck in the black of night. Hard men in rubber boots, mean hooks slung over their shoulders, yell and argue in the artificial day of fluorescent lights. "How much? Whaddaya, kiddin' me?" The first light of morning strikes the old sheds.

Under the snaking highway on the fishy, cobbled street
lies a ten-foot shark. Fish boxes are scattered like fallen
building blocks.

Inside, giant tunas and mako sharks lie on their sides like beached battleships. Men fillet them as skillfully as surgeons. The halibut are bigger than doormats, the sturgeon look like alien life-forms. Red snapper and green dolphin, shellfish and cuttlefish, crayfish and carp. The trucks come, the fish go, all over the city, all over the country.

Morocco

RISSANI, NEAR ERFOUD

They come to the market at Rissani where, 1,200 years ago, the Arab city of Sijilmassa grew fat on riches brought from all over Africa—amber, gold, salt, and slaves.

They come from mud-walled towns that rise from the Tafilalet oasis like shoe boxes.

They come astride tiny donkeys that are almost hidden under the enormous loads they carry in saddle baskets: fruit and vegetables, grain and dates.

Through the great gate at Rissani, down narrow, dusty alleys come the overladen donkeys. *"Allez, allez! Attention, attention!"* Get out of the way or be knocked down. For two dirhams they leave their donkeys at the donkey park. At the end of the day, they are somehow able to find their own amid all the kicking, biting, and screaming.

Shafts of light crisscross the dusty dark in reed-covered souks. There are blocks of fat for making soap; folk medicines—dried chameleons, hedgehogs, porcupines, and owls; pottery; clothing; musk.

Berbers, Bedouin, and Tuareg (the "blue men" of the desert) crowd through the arched portals into walled souks, a different sale going on in each: donkeys, sheep, cattle. The traders haggle. There is never a fixed price here.

In the cattle souk, men crowded into tight bunches under the blazing sun argue over prices while their tiny, short-horned cattle wait patiently.

"No, no! You want a camel for a chicken price!" they shout, no matter what they're selling. "What is your *final* offer? I know you are poor, but you have a rich heart."

Date-laden donkeys muscle their way into the date souk, where the dates are as numerous as the flies. Buyers in hooded djellabas hold fat dates in their cupped palms, separating the fruit from the pit with their thumbs.

Beyond the town, beyond the oasis, at the edge of the vast Sahara, rise the great dunes at Merzouga, glowing in the red afternoon light. Eight hundred feet high, they curl in sharp ridges and crests like a giant tidal wave that on a whim might bury the oasis, the town, and the market forever.

The painting on the cover of this book
is of a flower market in Ambato, Ecuador.
The painting on the title page is of a donkey
parking lot in Zagora, Morocco.

*The illustrations in this book were done in Winsor Newton watercolors on
500 pound Strathmore Bristol.
The display type was set in Mogadishu. The text was set in Meridien.
Printed and bound by Tien Wah Press. Production supervision by Bonnie King.*

*Lothrop, Lee & Shepard Books, a division of William Morrow & Company, Inc.,
1350 Avenue of the Americas, New York, New York 10019.
Printed in Singapore.
First Edition   1 2 3 4 5 6 7 8 9 10
Library of Congress Cataloging in Publication Data
Lewin, Ted. Market! / by Ted Lewin.
p.   cm. Summary: Describes, in simple text and illustrations, the special
characteristics of different types of markets throughout the world, from the
Fulton Fish Market in New York to Durbar Square, Patan, where
temples rise like pagodas behind the flute sellers.
ISBN 0-688-12161-6. — ISBN 0-688-12162-4 (lib. bdg.)
1. Markets—Juvenile literature. [1. Markets.] I. Title.
HF5470.L48 1996   381'.18—dc20 95-7439 CIP AC*